Let It Find Me Ready

Gia

Published by Rooted Hound Publishing

© 2025 by Gia

ISBN: 978-1-969687-06-8

Printed in the United States of America

For the ones who will one day read these words and understand—

love was the lesson all along.

Table of Contents

Before You Begin

You don't have to read this book straight through. You can open it anywhere—on a quiet morning, a restless night, or in the middle of a moment you can't name—and you'll find what your soul is ready to hear.

Each chapter is a conversation, each practice a pause. Read slowly. Let the white space do its work.

You might cry, you might smile, you might remember something you didn't know you forgot. That's how it's meant to be.

This isn't a book about endings. It's a book about living unafraid of them. You don't need to understand everything right now. You just need to breathe.

The rest will find you when it's time.

Preface

There was a time I thought readiness meant having everything in order—the plans, the lists, the binders, the what-ifs. I thought being prepared would save me from the ache of uncertainty. But the more I tried to control life, the more I realized: fear can wear a thousand disguises, and control is one of them.

This book isn't about the end of the world. It's about the end of fear. It's about remembering that every ending— whether of a day, a life, a season, or a story—is only another doorway back to love. We are not here to perfect our safety plans. We are here to soften into presence.

The truth is, we all die a thousand little deaths before the final one. We die to old versions of ourselves. We die to illusions of permanence. We die to the idea that love can be lost. And every one of those deaths is practice. Not for despair—but for peace.

To live ready is to live awake. To love now is to be unafraid later. To breathe deeply in this moment is to remember that we are eternal.

So, if you came to these pages searching for how to survive, I hope you find something gentler: how to *be*. How to meet each ending with grace. How to make peace not someday, but now.

Because readiness isn't about what we store—it's about what we surrender.

And maybe that's what all of us are here to learn.

Part I — Remembering Why We Came

Before birth, we knew the way. We only came to remember it.

Chapter 1 — The Contract We Signed

"Before I was born, I knew everything. And then I chose to forget."

There is a place beyond this world. A place where time does not tick and bodies are not worn. Where you don't walk—you remember. You don't fear—you know. And you are not small—you are whole. It's there you stood before this life began. Maybe you were with your guide— one you've traveled with many times. Or maybe your great-grandmother was there, smiling like she never left. Maybe Jesus stood beside you. Maybe Thoth. Maybe a light so bright you didn't need to ask who it was.

You were surrounded by love. Wrapped in wisdom. And you—you were asked: "Are you ready?" Not to be punished. Not to suffer for some forgotten sin. But to grow. To remember. To return, one slow step at a time, to the truth you never really left. And so, with every ounce of courage and clarity you had, you said yes. You sat at the table and wrote your story.

You picked your birthday. The body. The bloodline. The town you'd call home. You picked the people who would love you—and the ones who would break you open. You chose your challenges like a gardener picks soil: "This one will help me grow compassion." "This one will teach me to forgive." "This pain...I'll carry it, so I can help others carry theirs." You chose when you would come in. And yes—you chose when you might leave.

Not always in one fixed way. There are exit points—forks in the road your soul can choose from, depending on the lessons you've fulfilled. But one way or another, you knew: "I won't be there forever."

The book of life you wrote was never a prison. It was a promise. And then...you closed the book. You passed through the veil. And you forgot. You forgot the contract. You forgot the courage. You forgot you said yes. And life began.

You were born into a world of noise and rules. Where babies are held for a moment and then taught how to fear. Where pain is proof of punishment. Where death is taboo.

Where joy is earned and safety is sold. And yet—even with all that forgetting—something inside you remembers. In the quiet. In dreams. In that unshakable sense that you were meant to be here, now, even if you don't know why.

You've felt it, haven't you? That pull in your gut. That whisper of "there's more than this." That strange peace in moments of chaos, like your soul has seen this before. You're not crazy. You're remembering. This chapter—this life—it isn't random. You chose it. And no matter how chaotic this world becomes, that truth will always anchor you: "I am not a victim of fate. I am a soul keeping a promise."

You didn't forget because you were weak. You forgot because forgetting was the rule of the game. If you recalled everything—the safety, the love, the reasons—you wouldn't remain. You'd float. You'd yearn for home. You wouldn't risk pain if you remembered how it ends. And so...you entered the forgetting.

You were born into a world where pain can feel permanent and time moves like a weight. Where bills come due and children cry, and the sky sometimes looks like it's falling. You were born into a body that breaks. A family that doesn't always understand. A system that tells you to be quiet, behave, fit in. And so—slowly—you began to believe it: that life happens to you, that some people get lucky and others suffer, that death is the worst thing that could happen. You stopped feeling eternal and started feeling afraid.

But here's the sacred paradox: even in the forgetting, the truth is still there. Buried deep beneath your habits and your hurts is the memory of your soul. Every moment of déjà vu. Every whisper in the dark that says, "This isn't the end." Every impossible synchronicity. Every tear that falls with purpose. These are the breadcrumbs you left for yourself. You knew it would be hard. You knew you'd doubt it all. So you placed signposts in your path. That quote that shattered your heart open. That dream that felt too real to ignore. That book that fell off the shelf right when you needed it. You left those for yourself.

Even your most significant pain might have been part of the plan. Not because you deserve it—it is never that. But

4

because you chose a soul curriculum with depth. Because you knew you could alchemize even the darkest chapters into wisdom.

"Why would I choose such a hard path?" Because you knew you could help others through theirs. Because your soul was ready to grow. Because love—true love—doesn't just seek comfort. It seeks expansion.

There is no shame in forgetting. The world is loud. Trauma is heavy. Fear is sticky. But you are remembering now. And that changes everything. Not the events, maybe. Not the way the world spins. But the way you move through it— with sacred awareness, with quiet peace, with a thread running through your being that says: "I chose this. And I am remembering why."

Pause & Consider

- Does any part of your life feel "chosen," even if you can't explain why?

- What breadcrumbs—synchronicities, quotes, dreams—have shown up right when you needed them?

Journaling Prompt

"Before I came here, I chose…"
Write freely. No editing. Let memory—not logic—
answer.

Soul Reflection

There are moments I still wonder why I said yes. When the
ache feels too heavy, when the world tilts toward chaos, I
question the contract I once wrote with so much courage.
But then, in the smallest ways, I remember—the scent of
rain on warm soil, the laughter of someone I love, the hush
that falls just before sunrise. In those moments, I feel the
echo of that original agreement: *I will go. I will grow. I will
love.* Maybe readiness isn't about having no fear at all.
Maybe it's about knowing that even here—inside this
fragile human story—I am still the same soul who said yes.
And I would say it again.

Interlude: Letter to My Soul

My beloved soul,

I'm beginning to understand that I didn't come here to be perfect. I came here to *feel.* To stumble. To question. To forget—and then remember.

For so long, I thought being human meant getting everything right: making no mistakes, saying the perfect words, staying calm when the world was loud. But I see it now. You didn't send me here for perfection. You sent me here for experience—for growth through the mess, through the ache, through the holy imperfection of living.

I'm sorry for the times I thought you abandoned me. For the nights I mistook silence for distance. You were never gone—you were waiting for me to listen again.

Every time I doubted myself, you were the quiet pulse beneath it—the breath that steadied me when I forgot how to breathe. Every act of love I offered, every forgiveness I finally gave, was you reminding me who I am.

I see now that nothing was wasted. Not the heartbreaks. Not the detours. Not the waiting. They were the curriculum we agreed to—the path that would teach compassion, patience, and presence.

So here I am. Learning to touch the earth again. Learning to laugh at my own trying. Learning that holiness isn't found in control—it's found in surrender.

If I forget again, please remind me gently. Remind me that I am both a student and a teacher. Remind me that every ending I fear is only another return to love.

I promise I'll keep walking, even when the way looks uncertain. I'll keep softening, even when it hurts. And when the time comes to return, I'll recognize you waiting at the threshold.

Until then, stay close. I'm listening now. And I am finally remembering.

With love,

The Human You Chose to Become

Chapter 2 — The Fear of Death

You didn't always fear death. No one does at first. Babies don't worry about dying. They live inside every breath, every giggle, every color and sound. Children don't obsess with time running out; they're too busy being alive. But something happens as we grow. The world starts whispering:

"Be careful."
"Don't fall."
"That could kill you."

And the soul that once said *yes* begins to doubt. Somewhere along the way, death becomes the enemy—the thing we don't talk about. The shadow we try to outrun with youth serums, seatbelts, bunkers, and distractions. We see it in movies as the end, in hospitals as failure, in obituaries as sadness. We read *gone too soon* no matter the age. But what if none of that is true? What if the real tragedy isn't death itself—but how little we live while we're here?

I think about my granddaughter sometimes. She's so young, so wise, so full of questions. But her little heart already carries fears that break mine. She won't take a bath without being afraid she'll slip and hit her head. She sees danger in the most innocent places. And I wonder—where did that come from? She wasn't born afraid. She was born knowing how to feel. But this world...this noisy, frightened world...taught her to fear before it taught her to trust. And she's not alone.

So many of us are walking around as adults still carrying the fears we picked up as kids. Fear of death. Fear of abandonment. Fear of pain. Fear of the dark—literal or spiritual. And the most dangerous part? Most of us don't even realize we're afraid. We call it *planning*. We call it *being realistic*. We call it *being careful*. But underneath, it's the same old fear: *What happens when this is over? Will it hurt? Will I vanish? Will I fail the people I love?*

Here's what I believe now—after everything: Death isn't a punishment. It's a transition. A change of costume. A return ticket. A homecoming.

I don't say that to make it sound easy. I say it because I've felt the truth deep in my bones. You don't stop existing when the body does. Your consciousness continues. You are not the body. You are *inside* it—wearing it, loving it, learning through it. But when the time comes…you'll slip it off like a coat you've outgrown.

Fear of death grows when we forget who we are. Once you remember that you wrote the ending before the beginning, that you chose your exit point with care, that you will never lose everything—only the illusion of everything—death stops being a monster. It becomes a mystery. One we'll all one day solve, together.

Maybe fear was never about death itself. Maybe it was about the parts of life we never allowed ourselves to live.

We call death the great unknown, but isn't every tomorrow unknown? We fear its finality, yet we spend whole years numbing ourselves to the present. We hide from change, from grief, from endings—and in doing so, we taste a little death every day.

What if dying isn't the enemy at all? What if it's the mirror that reminds us how to live?

When I finally stopped trying to outrun the thought of death, something softened. Colors grew brighter. Conversations became slower, truer. The small things— the cup of tea, the laugh from another room, the feel of warm sunlight through the window—stopped being background noise and became sacred.

It's strange, isn't it? The more we make peace with dying, the more alive we become. Because fear isn't what keeps us here—love is. And love, when lived fully, doesn't vanish when the body does.

So maybe the invitation isn't to conquer fear, but to befriend it. To see it as a signal that life is precious. To let it point us back to gratitude.

If we can hold death in our hearts without despair, we might finally understand what every soul has always known: that life and death are not opposites—they are partners in the same dance.

We were never meant to live afraid. We were meant to live aware. That awareness doesn't dull life; it brightens it. It brings tenderness to the mundane. It makes your child's laughter feel eternal. It makes the sky feel like a love letter. It helps you let go—not recklessly, but peacefully.

So, when death does come—whether it's the end of this lifetime or just the end of a chapter—we can meet it without panic. With grace. With gratitude for the story we've lived, and for the promise that continues beyond it.

To make peace with death is to make peace with life itself. It's to see that every breath is a beginning, and every ending is an opening back to where we started.

And maybe that's the greatest act of readiness there is.

Pause & Consider

- When did death first become *real* to you? Was it through a loss, a movie, a moment of fear?

- How do you think your early ideas about death shaped the way you live today?

Journaling Prompt

"If I were no longer afraid of death, I would…"
Write without censoring. Let honesty lead.

Companion Reflection

Sit quietly for a moment and imagine this: You are at peace—not because everything is certain, but because you no longer need it to be. There is love in your breath, softness in your body, and gratitude in your heart for the life still moving through you. Let that awareness settle like sunlight in your chest.

This is what readiness feels like. Not escape. Not control. Just love—steady, unhurried, unafraid.

Soul Reflection

Before we were born, we promised to remember. Not through words, but through the ache of missing something we couldn't name. Every time we loved deeply, every time we lost, every time we paused long enough to listen—we remembered a little more. We came here to feel the beauty of being fragile, to rediscover strength inside the soft places. The soul doesn't rush the remembering. It unfolds in its own time, in its own quiet way. Trust that even when you forget, life is still guiding you back to what you already know: you are loved, you are guided, and you are never alone.

Part II — Living Between Control and Surrender

Peace begins where control ends. Love begins where surrender begins.

Chapter 3 — The Illusion of Control

We prepare. We plan. We make lists, check batteries, refill prescriptions, and put things in their proper places because movement feels like safety. Because order feels like peace. Because when life feels uncertain, doing something feels better than doing nothing.

And sometimes—it is. There's wisdom in being ready. There's strength in caring for what we can. But beneath all that planning hums a quieter question: *Am I preparing from fear…or from love?*

Control is one of the oldest illusions we cling to. We convince ourselves that if we just work harder, plan better, or anticipate every possible outcome, we can avoid pain. We can sidestep loss. We can keep the people we love safe forever.

But life—this wild, sacred, unpredictable life—was never meant to be managed. Not the timing of our birth. Not the moment of our death. Not the weather, the outcomes, or the hearts of others.

We can guide, but not command. We can prepare, but not predict. And the more we grip, the more we suffer.

I've lived in that place—the white-knuckled holding-on, afraid that if I loosened my grip, everything I loved would slip away. But there comes a moment when you realize: *Control is not the same as care. Control is not the same as love.*

You can care deeply without clinging. You can love fiercely without managing every detail.

We think control keeps us safe, but often it only keeps us anxious. It tells us we can never rest. It convinces us that the world will fall apart if we stop watching it for one second. It traps our hearts in a loop of *what if.*

Control feels productive, but it can quietly steal our joy. While you're counting, you might miss the laughter. While you're calculating, you might miss the sunrise. While you're guarding, you might forget to feel.

This chapter isn't an invitation to stop caring—it's an invitation to care differently. To trade the illusion of control for the truth of trust. To move from fear-driven doing to love-led being.

Because the most powerful moments in life—birth, healing, forgiveness, love—aren't controlled. They're surrendered to.

You are not here to master certainty. You are here to master peace.

Control whispers, "If you let go, everything will fall apart." But trust answers, "If I let go, everything might finally fall into place."

When I loosened my grip, life didn't crumble; it softened. My breath deepened. My body exhaled. And I realized that readiness built on fear was exhausting, but readiness built on faith felt like peace.

We can still plan, still prepare, still take care of what matters. But now we do it with open hands instead of closed fists. That's the difference between living afraid of loss and living awake to love.

Pause & Consider

- Where in your life are you still holding on too tightly?
- What might happen if you loosened your grip just a little—and trusted life to meet you halfway?

Journaling Prompt

"If I stopped trying to control everything, I would…"
Let your heart finish the sentence.

Practice: The Open-Hands Exercise

Find a quiet moment and sit where you can be undisturbed.
Rest your hands in your lap, palms facing down. Feel their
weight—the small tension that gathers when we hold too
tightly.

Now turn your palms upward. Let them rest open, without
effort.

Notice the shift. The simple act of opening your hands
changes your breath, your posture, your mind.

With your hands open, say softly (aloud if you can): "I can
care without controlling. I can love without clinging. I can
prepare without fear."

Take a slow inhale. As you exhale, imagine releasing one small thing you've been trying to manage—a worry, a person, a plan. Let it rest in the hands of something greater than yourself.

Stay here for a few breaths, palms open, trusting that what's meant for you will never need to be forced. When you're ready, place one hand over your heart. Whisper:

"I am held. Even when I let go."

Then return to your day, carrying that quiet ease with you.

Chapter 4 — Trying Anyway

So here we are. We know we can't control the storm. We know death is part of the design. We remember that we chose this life—this path, this timing, even this end.

And still…we try.

We store the rice. We plant the seeds. We fill the gas cans and label the bins. We write the phone tree. We build the binder.

Because love still lives in these hands. Because the soul said yes, but the body still wants to protect. Because we're human—and trying is what we do.

This is where surrender meets effort, where wisdom holds hands with instinct. Where we quietly say: "I will not panic. But I will still prepare. I will not cling. But I will still care. I will not run from my contract. But I will show up for my family."

Trying doesn't mean we're afraid. It means we're alive.

We try not to change the ending. We try to walk toward it with grace. There's a softness to this kind of effort—it's not the frantic energy of survivalism, but the quiet steadiness of devotion.

I don't prep because I'm terrified. I prep because I love deeply. Because I want to hold the ones I love through whatever comes next—whether it's a solar flare, a power outage, or a hard winter of the soul.

We try...not to stop death, but to walk each other home with dignity. Some might call it prepping. And maybe it is. But I don't do it with panic in my bones or doom in my heart. I do it because I care. Because I want to ease suffering where I can.

I'm not preparing to outwit fate—I'm preparing to meet it with grace. I'm not trying to stockpile control. I'm trying to stay rooted in who I am, no matter what comes.

Trying without attachment is the middle path. "I will plant the garden…But I release whether it grows." "I will store the food…But I'll decide whether I'll need it." "I will write the will, the plan, the goodbye letter…But I'll decide whether I'll leave early or stay long."

This is spiritual maturity. Not giving up. Not checking out. But showing up with open hands and a steady heart.

You are not foolish for trying. You are not weak for hoping. You are not wasting your time.

Trying is not about proving anything. It's about participating in your own becoming. It's the quiet, human way we say: *I'm still here. I still care. I choose love anyway.*

And maybe that's what readiness really looks like—not perfection, but presence. Not control, but compassion in motion. Not fear, but faith that love is still worth the effort.

Pause & Consider

- Can you feel the difference between trying from fear and trying from love?
- How might your daily actions change if you let love, not anxiety, guide your preparation?

Journaling Prompt

"I am preparing not because I'm afraid, but because…"

Let your soul fill in the blank and show you what readiness means for you.

Interlude: Letter to My Children (for When I'm Gone)

My Dearest Children,

If you're reading this one day when I'm no longer here in the way you've always known me, I need you to remember this first: I never really left.

The love that raised you isn't buried; it's multiplied. It lives in your laugh, in the way you care for others, in the quiet things you do without thinking. Every time you reach for kindness instead of fear, I'm there. Every time you find wonder in something ordinary, I'm smiling through you.

Please don't fill your days with "what ifs." You don't have to wonder if I'm proud—I always was. You don't have to regret what we didn't say—love says it endlessly in the space between words. And you don't have to be afraid of death. It's just the moment I step into another room.

When you miss me, do something gentle for the world. Plant something. Feed something. Forgive someone. That's how we stay connected—through love in motion.

I don't want you to spend your life preparing for loss. I want you to spend it preparing for joy—for the small, holy moments that make it all worthwhile. Don't waste time chasing perfection. Just be present. Laugh even when it rains. Remember how we used to stop for the ducks, or the sunsets, or just because something felt right. Keep doing that. Always.

If I could tell you one last thing, it would be this: You are stronger than you know, softer than you think, and more loved than you could ever imagine.

And when your time comes to cross that threshold, don't be afraid. I'll be waiting—just a breath away, just beyond the light. Until then, live. Live fully, honestly, and wide awake.

With all that I am,

Mom

Chapter 5 — When the Sky Breaks Open

The signs are everywhere now, not just in the world, but in our lives. The seasons of certainty are shifting. The air feels different, and so do we. Something is changing—something we can't quite name.

Some call it awakening. Some call it loss. Some call it rebirth. Maybe it's all of it. Maybe it's none. But most of us can feel it: life itself is holding its breath.

There are days when the data of our lives looks terrifying—the test results, the bills, the headlines, the silence that follows news we didn't expect. We trace the patterns, search for answers, check the numbers, and watch for signs. And some mornings we stare at the horizon and whisper, *"Not yet…please, not yet."*

But this chapter isn't about what might fall apart. It's about what will always remain.

Your soul. Your stillness. Your ability to stay rooted when everything around you is shifting.

Because no matter what changes outside of you, there is something unbreakable inside of you.

It's not easy. Even the most grounded person can feel the static in the air—the tension before a decision, the ache before a goodbye, the quiet fear before a leap of faith. We weren't built to hold this much unknown. And yet, we are holding it.

Somehow, we are still rising. Still making tea. Still saying *I love you*. Still showing up for one another. Still breathing through the storm.

That is sacred.

Change will come—the ending, the diagnosis, the heartbreak, the new beginning. But let it find me ready— not just with plans and preparations, but with peace in my chest.

Let it find me grounded enough to say: "Yes, I saw it coming. But I also saw my soul." "Yes, I felt afraid. But I was not fear."

If the sky breaks open, let it break me open too—to love more deeply, to live more vividly, to remember who I am—not just as a body, but as a being made of light and memory and eternity.

You don't have to know the outcome to be the calm. You just have to remember that calm is your original state.

Maybe the invitation has never been to predict the storm, but to prepare the heart—to let every change remind us how sacred it is to be here, alive, awake, unafraid to feel it all.

Because readiness isn't about surviving the storm. It's about letting it reveal what was indestructible all along.

Pause & Consider

- What "storm" in your life has taught you the most about who you are?
- What would it look like to let change open you instead of close you?

Practice: The Center of the Storm

Find a quiet spot where you can sit comfortably. Close your eyes and take a slow breath in through your nose. Let it travel deep into your belly. Hold it for a count of three. Then exhale gently through your mouth, letting your shoulders fall.

Repeat this three times. With each breath, imagine the world around you softening.

Now, picture yourself standing at the center of a great open field. The wind begins to rise. You can hear it moving through the trees. But as the air swirls, notice that right where you stand—the very center—there is stillness. The wind moves around you, not through you.

Whisper softly: "I am the calm. I am the stillness inside the change."

Stay here for a few moments. Let any thoughts or worries pass by like clouds. If emotions arise, don't chase them. Simply breathe and let them move through.

When you're ready, open your eyes. Touch your heart and remind yourself: "No matter what shifts, peace is home, and I can return to it anytime."

Carry that awareness into whatever the day brings.

Soul Reflection

Somewhere between control and surrender lies peace. It doesn't shout. It hums softly beneath the noise, waiting for us to notice. We weren't meant to master life—we were meant to meet it. To tend to what we can and release what we can't. Every breath is a conversation between effort and grace. When we stop fighting the current, the river begins to carry us toward exactly where we're meant to go. You don't have to let go of everything—just loosen your grip enough to let love steer.

Part III — The Heart Remembers

The heart is the oldest traveler of them all—it remembers every home we've ever known.

Chapter 6 — The Calm Within the Change

There will be people who panic. People who freeze. People who laugh until it's too late. People who scream. People who look to you.

And in those moments, there will be a choice: to be consumed by the chaos…or to become the calm.

This doesn't mean you'll have all the answers. It doesn't mean you'll never feel afraid. It means that when fear rises, you know where to go: inward. To that quiet, unshaken part of you that remembers who you are. To the soul that knows you've been through change before—and survived every version of it.

You are not here only to endure. You are here to embody peace in motion.

You may have already felt it: in a crisis, something inside you slows down. While others lose themselves, you find your breath. You become the steady voice, the quiet hands, the one who notices the next right step. This isn't a coincidence. You were made for this.

There is a calm that can only be cultivated *before* the change comes. Not through denial. Not through pretending everything will stay the same. But through remembering who you are when you're not reacting. Through sitting with your own vulnerability and making peace with it. Through crying when it's time to cry—and then standing back up with love still in your chest.

This calm is not cold. It's not robotic. It's not about perfection or pretending you're fine. It's fierce. It's compassionate. It's rooted. It feels everything—but doesn't drown in it. It's the stillness that comes from trust.

Being '*the calm*' doesn't make you better than anyone else. It just means you've practiced presence a little longer. You've learned to pause before speaking. To breathe before reacting. To listen before deciding. And maybe that's why you're here now—not to lead with authority, but to steady with presence.

So, when others cry…let them. When they rage…stay soft. When they spin…breathe.

Not because it's easy, but because someone must hold the ground. And maybe your soul volunteered long ago to be that ground.

Let this be your mantra, whispered into the heart of any storm: "I am not the fear. I am not the noise. I am *'the calm.'* I am the center. I am the anchor."

And the quiet miracle is this: sometimes your stillness will save someone else. Not your logic. Not your plan. Just your presence.

That's what readiness really is—not the absence of fear, but the presence of peace strong enough to stay steady through it.

To be *'the calm'* within the change is to remember that peace is not the reward for safety—it's the way through uncertainty itself.

Pause & Consider

- Who do you become when others are falling apart?
- What does your calm look like—not the imagined perfect version, but the real one?
- How might you practice being *'that calm'* for yourself first?

Practice: The Centering Breath

When the world feels loud, find a still place within yourself. You don't need silence around you—only presence inside you.

1. **Sit or stand tall.** Feel your feet on the floor or the weight of your body on the chair. Let gravity hold you.

2. **Place one hand on your chest and one on your stomach.** Inhale slowly through your nose for a count of four. Feel your belly rise beneath your hand.

3. **Exhale through your mouth for a count of six.** Let your shoulders drop. Let your jaw unclench. Feel the exhale as release.

4. **Repeat this three times.** With each breath, imagine your heartbeat syncing with the steady rhythm of the earth beneath you.

Whisper softly:

"I am the calm within the change. I am anchored in peace."

When your mind starts to race, place your focus back on your heartbeat. It's proof that stillness and movement can coexist—just like peace and change.

Carry this breath with you into your next moment. It will always lead you home.

Chapter 7 — You're Not Crazy, You're Remembering

You start noticing things. The way the air feels different before a storm. The hum in your body when the sun flares. The moments when a word, a number, or a dream won't leave you alone.

You begin hearing whispers beneath the noise—truths you can't prove but somehow know. And part of you wonders, *"Am I losing it?"* No. You're remembering.

There is a kind of awakening that doesn't shout. It doesn't demand a stage or a following. It arrives quietly—like mist curling through a forest you didn't realize you'd planted. You don't wake up one day and suddenly become enlightened. You start noticing the thread—the golden one—woven through everything.

That déjà vu that feels more like a breadcrumb. That gut feeling that turns out to be right—again. That gentle pause when your heart whispers, *"I've done this before."*

You're not imagining it. You're remembering yourself. You're peeling back the layers of conditioning and fear and returning to the soul that has always been here. This isn't delusion. It's design. You're waking up inside the dream.

Sometimes remembering looks like sudden insight. Sometimes it looks like grief. Sometimes it feels like distance—pulling away from what no longer fits, outgrowing beliefs that once felt like home.

It can be lonely. It can be tender. It can feel like unraveling. But you're not unraveling—you're realigning.

You're not becoming someone new. You're becoming who you were before "*the forgetting.*"

People may not understand. They might call you too sensitive, too distracted, too intense, too *different.* But they're not the ones feeling the shift in their bones. They're not the ones waking in the middle of the night with your heart racing and no idea why. They're not the ones sensing the unseen connections, the patterns, the quiet call to come home.

You are. Because you're remembering the assignment. You're remembering the contract. You're remembering the truth.

Your intuition isn't a malfunction—it's a compass. It's your soul speaking through the static. And the more you listen, the clearer it becomes. The louder it gets. Until one day, the whispers turn into knowing.

And in that moment, you realize: "I am not crazy. I am not alone. I am not broken. I am remembering."

That's all awakening really is—not learning something new but recognizing what was always there.

When you begin to remember, life doesn't suddenly become easy. It becomes *real.* You stop chasing proof and start trusting presence. You stop explaining yourself and start listening to your own heart. And somehow, without trying, you begin to glow again.

Because remembering doesn't pull you out of the world, it roots you deeper into it—awake, aware, and finally at peace with being human.

Pause & Consider

- What have you been feeling lately that others might not understand?
- What part of you are you finally starting to trust— even if you can't explain it yet?

Interlude: Whispers of the Soul

You are not late.

You are not lost.

You are remembering in perfect time.

You came here to forget—so that remembering would feel like sunrise.

Every ache has been an awakening.

Every detour, a doorway.

Every pause, a prayer.

You are not here to find the light.

You *are* the light.

You are here to feel what it's like to carry it through the dark.

Do not rush.

Do not fix.

Just listen.

The whisper you've been hearing is not madness—it's memory. The soft call of home is woven through every breath you take.

And when the noise fades, you'll hear it clearly again:

"You are safe. You are loved. You are already home."

Chapter 8 — Death is Not the End

Death isn't the end. It never was. It's the doorway—the returning—the exhale after the longest breath you've ever taken.

We treat death as the opposite of life, but it isn't. It's the opposite of *birth*. And both are simply thresholds between worlds.

Some people think death is darkness—a vanishing, an erasure. But the truth is gentler than that. It isn't an ending—it's a releasing. A loosening of this heavy skin. A soft dissolving of name, weight, schedule, and pain. And underneath it all, what remains is *you*.

The real you. The one who existed before this life. The one who will exist after it. The soul that has done this many times before and will do it again, in love.

There are things we can't fully understand from here. The veil exists for a reason. But there are also things we can *feel*—deeply, instinctively—when we stop fearing them.

I don't believe death is punishment. I don't think it's random. And I don't believe it means we failed. I believe it's written with care into our story.

And I believe that the people we've lost are not gone. They're simply farther along. They walked ahead, as they were meant to. And when it's our time, we'll recognize their faces like we never missed a day.

When we stop seeing death as the end, something inside us shifts. We begin to live differently—softer, slower, more awake. We stop trying to beat the clock and start learning to dance with it. We hold our loved ones closer—not because we fear losing them, but because we finally feel the sacredness of this moment.

We prepare without panic. We breathe without rushing. We let go more easily. Because we know there is more than this.

That doesn't mean death is painless. The grief is real. The ache of losing someone you love is a season that refuses to change. But grief is not proof that death is bad—it's proof that love existed and still does.

Because love doesn't die when bodies do, love was never of the body. It moves through time, through space, through lifetimes. You are still loved by the ones who left. You always will be.

If my death comes tomorrow, I want to meet it with open hands. Not because I'm finished living, but because I've stopped resisting what I've always known: I am not the body. I am not this name. I am not '*this chapter.*'

I am the soul beneath it all. I am the story still being written. I am eternal.

When we truly know that, even endings feel gentle. Even loss becomes a kind of doorway. And death—rather than something to dread—becomes a remembering.

The soul doesn't fear death. It only hopes we'll live deeply enough that when the moment comes, we'll recognize it as a homecoming.

Pause & Consider

- What would shift for you if you saw death as a return instead of an ending?
- What would you do differently if you trusted that love is never lost?

Practice: The Gentle Goodbye

Find a quiet space where you can sit or lie down comfortably. Take a slow, deep breath in. Hold it for a moment… then exhale softly.

Close your eyes and imagine someone or something you've lost. It could be a person, a place, a version of yourself—

anything that still tugs at your heart. Picture it gently, not to relive the pain, but to bring it into the light.

Now place your hand over your heart. Whisper quietly: "Thank you for walking with me. Thank you for what you gave. Thank you for what remains."

Feel that gratitude expand in your chest. It's warm. Alive. Real. Let it soften whatever ache still lingers there.

When you're ready, imagine that person, place, or memory surrounded by a soft golden light. You don't have to send it away. Just let it rest—peaceful, whole, safe.

Take another slow breath and whisper: "I release the fear of losing what cannot be lost. Love is still here. Love is forever."

Stay with that feeling for a few breaths. When you open your eyes, notice how quiet the room feels. That stillness? That's presence. That's love without a form.

Carry that calm with you through the day. Each time you feel grief rise again, place your hand on your heart and return to those words:

"Love is still here."

Soul Reflection

The heart is a memory keeper. Long after the mind forgets, the heart still knows the feel of laughter, the warmth of presence, the sound of someone's name whispered in gratitude. The heart remembers what the world teaches us to ignore: that joy is holy, that grief is sacred, that love never ends. When we stop trying to protect the heart and instead let it breathe, we remember what living really is. The heart doesn't need to be healed—it just needs permission to stay open.

Part IV — Living Ready

Readiness is not waiting. It's living as if peace already belongs to you.

Chapter 9 — Dancing in the Rain

We didn't have a plan. Just a car, a day off, and a deep ache to give our kids something to remember. We didn't have money for a vacation. We barely had enough for gas. But we went anyway.

We drove west—out of routine, into something softer. And when we saw the sign for **Bushkill Falls**, we looked at each other and said, *"Why not?"*

We didn't have cameras. No cell phone to take photos. No towel, no snacks, no agenda. Just our kids' hands in ours and a trail that led us down to the roar of the falls.

We were fully present. No distractions. Just us and the sound of water pounding over ancient rock.

And then—the sky opened. Not a drizzle. Not a polite warning. A *deluge*. Like a cosmic bucket had been turned upside down.

We ran, soaking, slipping, laughing—our children squealing like it was the best thing that had ever happened. And maybe it was. Because in that moment, we weren't stressed. We weren't broke. We weren't worried about tomorrow. We were simply *alive.*

We stood there, sopping wet inside the gift shop. I used the last of our credit to buy us each a dry t-shirt. The sun came out. We sat on a bench feeding ducks and sharing popcorn.

That was it. That was the vacation. And I've never forgotten it.

Because we were together. Because we didn't resist the storm. Because we laughed through what could have ruined the day.

That's what this chapter is about. Not avoiding the rain—but learning to dance inside it.

There will always be something uncertain. Something undone. Something changing. But joy isn't found in everything being perfect. It's found in being *present* with what is.

Even if what is…is soaking wet, chaotic, messy, and real.

Joy is a radical act when the world feels heavy. It's how we defy despair. It's how we remember we're still human. It's how we honor the life we were given—even when it hurts.

Joy doesn't mean denial. It means choosing love anyway. It means laughing through the thunder. It means noticing the ducks. It means letting the sun hit your face the minute the clouds part—even if they come back again.

The world may never slow down. The plans may never be perfect. But today—this moment—you're here. And that's enough.

Maybe the secret isn't to find peace *after* the storm, but to let it find you *in* the storm. To let joy be your umbrella, and love your shelter.

The world might change tomorrow. But today? Today I laughed. Today I loved. Today I bought us all a dry t-shirt with the last of my credit, and I don't regret it for a second.

Because I was there. And that's what I'll take with me when I go.

Pause & Consider

- What is a moment in your life that cost very little—but meant everything?
- What might happen if you stopped waiting for peace to come after the storm…and started letting it show up *in the middle of it?*

Practice: The Joy in the Ordinary

Take a quiet walk through your home, your yard, or your favorite place. No music. No phone. Just presence. As you move, whisper softly: "Show me what's still good." Then, notice. Really notice.

The way light touches a wall. The smell of coffee cooling on the counter. The hum of the refrigerator, steady as a heartbeat. The softness of a pet's fur, the rhythm of your own breathing.

Joy doesn't shout. It hums. It lives in these small, ordinary places. The more you notice, the louder it becomes.

When something makes you smile, pause there. Let it fill you for a few breaths. Let your shoulders drop. Let your heart say, *thank you*.

This is the practice: not chasing joy, but receiving it. Not demanding more, but seeing what's already here.

And if you can, end the practice by whispering: "Even here, I am blessed. Even now, I am alive."

That's what it means to dance in the rain.

Chapter 10 — When the Pictures Fade

I don't have a single photo from that day at Bushkill Falls. No proof that we were there. No image to post or frame. Just a feeling. A memory that lives somewhere deeper than digital.

And yet, I remember everything. The wet hair. The kids' laughter. The way the sun came out right after we surrendered to the rain. I don't need a picture—because I was *present*.

Somewhere along the way, we started believing that life doesn't count unless it's documented. We take pictures of sunsets instead of watching them. We post our joy before we feel it. We record moments we're not even in—just to prove we were there. But the soul doesn't need evidence. It just needs *presence*.

The most sacred moments of our lives might never be seen by anyone else. The silent forgiveness whispered in the mirror. The breath you take before saying, *I'm sorry*. The small kindness no one notices. The decision to stay calm when it would be easier to shout. The moment you chose love when fear was louder.

These are the moments that shape you. Not the grand gestures. Not the curated milestones. But the invisible choices to stay, soften, and show up.

No one may ever know how many times you've chosen peace over panic. How often you've sat quietly with your pain instead of numbing it? How many storms you've walked through with grace instead of noise? But you know. And your soul keeps the record.

One day, if everything goes dark—if the grid goes down, if the pictures fade, if the stories vanish—what will remain is this truth: "I was there. And I felt it. And that was enough."

We weren't sent here to *perform* life. We were sent here to *live* it. To taste it. To cry through it. To laugh in the rain without needing proof it ever happened.

So if no one sees your joy—feel it anyway. If no one applauds your healing—do it anyway. If no one documents your peace—hold it anyway.

Because the most important parts of your story will never be captured. They'll be *embodied*. And that's more than enough.

Pause & Consider

- When was the last time you were fully present in a moment—without trying to capture it?
- What would life feel like if you were the witness you most wanted to impress?

Practice: The Unrecorded Moment

Choose one small, ordinary moment today—morning coffee, the walk to the mailbox, folding a towel, watching light move across a wall.

Don't take a picture. Don't reach for your phone. Just *be there*.

Notice everything: the texture, the scent, the sound, the temperature of the air. Let your senses gather what the camera never could.

Feel your breath moving through you. Feel time slowing, stretching, softening.

Whisper quietly: "I am here. I am alive. This moment belongs to my soul."

Stay until you feel it—that subtle shift from observer to participant. That's presence. That's living.

When you move on with your day, carry this truth with you: You don't need to capture beauty to keep it. When you *feel* it fully, it's already yours.

Chapter 11 — Make Peace Now

There's always something unresolved. A text you never answered. A conversation you never finished. A truth you were too afraid to speak. A softening you swore you'd get around to when things slowed down.

But life rarely slows down. And peace rarely waits.

If these past years have taught us anything, it's this: we don't always get a warning. We don't always get tomorrow. And the people we love won't always be here when we finally feel ready to love them well.

That's not meant to scare you. It's meant to *free* you.

Because if you knew the door might close tomorrow, you'd walk through it today.

Make peace now. Not later. Not once the bills are paid, or the house is clean, or the plan is perfect. Now.

Call the person. Write the letter. Speak the forgiveness. Loosen your grip. Apologize first. Say thank you. Say I love you.

Even if it feels clumsy. Even if it's not received the way you hope. Even if the only person who needs to hear it…is *you*.

Make peace with your body. It has carried you through so much—through heartbreak and healing, exhaustion and awe. Even if it's tired. Even if it's hurting. Even if it never looked or worked the way you wanted. It has shown up for you every single day. Make peace with it now.

Make peace with your past. With the versions of you who didn't know what you know now. With the roads you didn't take. With the people who couldn't love you well. They were part of the story. But they are not your ending.

Make peace with the waiting. With the uncertainty. With the things that never turned out the way you prayed they would. Because every unanswered prayer has carried a quiet protection, a hidden grace you might only see later.

And make peace with death—not in a morbid way, but in the sacred way of someone who finally understands that life is not guaranteed, and that every breath is a miracle.

You don't have to be ready to die. You only have to stop living like you're invincible.

Let peace meet you now. Let it wrap around you before you need it. Let it become the frequency you live from. Because peace isn't something you stumble into at the end. It's something you practice every day in how you love, forgive, and let go.

So if the sky breaks open—if the world shifts tomorrow—you won't need to search for peace. You'll already *be* it.

Pause & Consider

- Who or what is still taking up space in your heart?
- What would it look like to lay it down gently—not with blame, not with force, but with softness and finality?

Practice: The Soft Release

Find a quiet space and something to write with. At the top of a page, write: "What I'm still holding."

Then, without thinking too hard, begin to list what rises up. A name. A memory. A worry. An expectation. It might be small. It might be decades old. Just let it come.

When you're finished, place your hand over the words. Take a slow breath in through your nose. Exhale through your mouth.

Now read your list softly, one item at a time. And after each one, whisper: "I bless you. I release you. I set you free."

If tears come, let them. They are part of the release. You don't have to understand how forgiveness works. You only have to be willing.

When you're done, fold the paper. You can tear it, burn it, bury it, or simply keep it in a drawer. The action doesn't matter as much as the intention: You have chosen peace over perfection. End by placing a hand over your heart and saying:

"May what I've released find its healing. May what remains within me be light."

Then take one last deep breath. Feel how much easier it is to carry yourself now. That is the weight of peace.

Chapter 12 — And If I Stay

Not everyone will go. Some of us will stay. Not because we earned it. Not because we planned perfectly. But because our story continues—for now—on this side of the veil.

And if I stay…I want to live like it means something.

Maybe your soul contract doesn't end with this chapter. Maybe you're here to witness the rebuilding—of your life, your family, your faith, your joy. Maybe you're here to carry memory forward, to keep love moving through the world.

You don't have to know *why*. You just have to listen. When the silence settles, when the dust clears, when the old life fades away, you'll rise—not as the same person, but as the one who remembers.

If I stay…I want to grow food and teach others how. I want to tell stories around a fire and remind people who they are. I want to laugh again. I want to sing again. I want to take pain and turn it into prayer. I want to build a world that's rooted in truth—not fear, not greed, not control.

If I stay, I will not go back to sleep. We don't survive to survive. We survive to serve. To love deeper. To lead quieter. To walk beside those still finding their way.
Because survival without soul is just a slower kind of death. But survival with remembrance? That becomes legacy.

There will be others who are scared. Others who are angry. Others who never prepared, never believed, never thought it could change. You might be the only calm they see. The only story that still sounds like hope.

So if you're still here—if your lungs are breathing, if your heart is steady—don't waste it. Live it. Offer it. Root yourself in what's real. Hold out your hands and say, "We're still here. Let's begin again."

Maybe the ones who stay are the ones meant to rebuild heaven on earth. Not with systems, but with simplicity. With love. With memory. With soul.

Pause & Consider

- If your soul carries you through what's next, what kind of life do you want to live on the other side?
- What would it mean to stay—not just physically, but spiritually awake?

Soul Reflection

Readiness isn't a checklist. It's a state of grace. It's what happens when you stop waiting for life to begin and realize it already has. To live ready is to keep your hands open—to give, to receive, to release. It's to wake each morning knowing that whatever the day brings, you will meet it with love. Readiness isn't about expecting the end; it's about being fully alive now. When you live like that, every ending simply becomes another way of beginning again.

Practice: Living as Legacy

Find a quiet place where you can write or simply reflect. Take a deep breath and ask yourself: "If I stay, what do I want my life to teach?"

Close your eyes for a moment and let the answers come without editing. See yourself years from now—not as a survivor, but as a keeper of wisdom.

Who is around you? What kind of world are you helping to nurture? What do your days look like? What values guide you? What love continues through your hands?

Now, write a few lines beginning with: "If I stay, I will…"

Let it flow like a promise. It doesn't need to be perfect or poetic. Just true.

Maybe it's small things—planting a garden, making soup for a neighbor, showing someone they matter. Maybe it's big—teaching, creating, healing, building. Whatever it is, let it be rooted in love, not fear.

When you're finished, whisper:

"May the life I live become my offering. May what I build in love outlast my name."

Fold your words and keep them somewhere safe—in your journal, on your altar, in a pocket of your heart.

Every time you feel uncertain, read them again. They're not a to-do list. They're a reminder of why you stayed.

Epilogue — Let It Find Me Ready

I don't know what will come. Not exactly. None of us do.

We have signs, feelings, dreams, and quiet intuitions—timelines drawn in chalk on the edges of our calendars. We prepare. We hope. We pray.

But when it comes—whatever *it* is—I don't want to be frozen in fear. I want to be *ready*.

Not ready in the way the world defines it. Not with bunkers, maps, or twenty-year plans. Not with the illusion of control.

I want to be ready in my soul. Ready because I made peace with death. Ready because I softened into life. Ready because I remembered why I came. Ready because I stopped performing and started *being*.

Ready because I didn't waste my time hiding—I used it to love.

Ready because I forgave. Because I released. Because I laughed. Because I lived.

If the sky breaks open, let it find me with dirt on my hands from planting something that might never grow. Let it find me mid-laughter. Let it find me telling someone the truth. Let it find me whispering to the trees, or thanking the earth, or holding someone who needs to be held.

Let it find me already awake. Already peaceful. Already remembering.

And if nothing comes—if the world keeps spinning and the storm delays for another age—still, let me live like this.

Let me live like I was made for it. Let me live like I was meant to be here. Let me live like the soul I am—anchored, aware, and wide open.

Because either way, I came for a reason. And I'm not afraid anymore.

Final Reflection

Read this slowly. Out loud, if you can. Let the words settle in your bones:

"I chose this life. I prepared what I could. I released what I couldn't. I am not here to outrun the storm—I am here to become the stillness inside it. When the time comes…let it find me ready."

Afterword Blessing

May you meet each moment with open hands. May you remember that you were never meant to control life—only to walk with it. When change comes, may it find you soft, not shattered. When endings arrive, may they reveal the beginnings that have been waiting all along. May you never mistake fear for readiness, nor readiness for fear. And may the love that carried you into this world carry you home, again and again, in peace.

Author's Note

This book was never written to tell anyone how to live or what to believe. It began as a way to remind myself—to remember what I already knew but kept forgetting.

In the quiet hours, when the world felt uncertain, I found myself writing not about the end of anything, but about how to live unafraid of endings. Every chapter became a prayer, a conversation, a whisper from the part of me that still remembered peace.

If these words found you in a moment of loss or fear, may they help you breathe again. If they found you in stillness, may they help you see how sacred that is. And if they found you in the middle of your ordinary day, may they remind you that the ordinary is holy too.

Thank you for walking this path with me. May you always be ready—not because you've prepared for every possibility, but because you've learned to live fully in the one that's here.

— Gia

Acknowledgments

To everyone who has walked beside me through the long remembering—thank you.

To my husband, whose steady love anchors every page. To my family, for their faith, laughter, and patience as I build Rooted Hound Press one heartbeat at a time. To the readers who keep showing up with open hearts—your quiet messages and shared stories are what make this work feel like purpose.

And to the Soul that wrote this with me—thank you for reminding me that we are never really preparing for the end, only remembering how to begin again.

— *Gia*

For Your Own Journey

These pages are here for you to pause, to breathe, to listen to what your soul has been trying to say all along. You don't have to answer every question. Just let the words open a door inside you.

Reflection Prompts:

1. What moments recently made you feel most alive?
2. When do you feel closest to peace?
3. If you knew you were already ready, what would change?
4. Who or what helps you remember love when you forget?
5. Write one promise to yourself that begins, *"If I stay..."*

Notes from the Journey

You don't have to write anything here. You can simply sit for a moment, breathe, and listen for what's still echoing inside you. Sometimes, what follows a book isn't a thought—it's a silence that wants to be honored.

If something rises—words, memories, names, prayers—let it come. If nothing does, let that be your peace.

These pages are for you. For what you can't say out loud yet. For what you don't want to forget.

Also by Gia

From Rooted Hound Press

Returning to Wholeness: An Invitation to the Soul
Echoes Through the Spiral: A Soul's Continuum
Healing the Past Through the Present
Let It Find Me Ready

Pocket Sanctuaries

Whispers from the Soul
The Test I Refused—and Why That Was the Answer

In Development

Healing Yourself, Healing Your Soul: An Ayurvedic Journey Back to Wholeness
Layla and Lilly and the Dragonfly Guardians

www.ingramcontent.com/pod-product-compliance
Lightning Source LLC
LaVergne TN
LVHW051423080426
835508LV00022B/3222